# LIBRARIES

by Emma Bassier

**Cody Koala**

An Imprint of Pop!

popbooksonline.com

abdobooks.com
Published by Pop!, a division of ABDO, PO Box 398166, Minneapolis, Minnesota 55439. Copyright © 2020 by POP, LLC. International copyrights reserved in all countries. No part of this book may be reproduced in any form without written permission from the publisher. Pop!™ is a trademark and logo of POP, LLC.

Printed in the United States of America, North Mankato, Minnesota

052019
092019

**THIS BOOK CONTAINS RECYCLED MATERIALS**

Cover Photo: iStockphoto
Interior Photos: iStockphoto, 1, 5 (top), 5 (bottom left), 5 (bottom right), 7, 8, 9, 11, 13, 14, 16, 17, 21; Shutterstock Images, 19

Editor: Meg Gaertner
Series Designer: Jake Slavik

Library of Congress Control Number: 2018964601
Publisher's Cataloging-in-Publication Data
Names: Bassier, Emma, author.
Title: Libraries / by Emma Bassier.
Description: Minneapolis, Minnesota : Pop!, 2020 | Series: Places in my community | Includes online resources and index.
Identifiers: ISBN 9781532163494 (lib. bdg.) | ISBN 9781532164934 (ebook)
Subjects: LCSH: Libraries--Juvenile literature. | Library buildings--Juvenile literature. | Libraries and community--Juvenile literature.
Classification: DDC 027--dc23

## Hello! My name is

# Cody Koala

Pop open this book and you'll find QR codes like this one, loaded with information, so you can learn even more!

Scan this code* and others like it while you read, or visit the website below to make this book pop.

### popbooksonline.com/libraries

*Scanning QR codes requires a web-enabled smart device with a QR code reader app and a camera.

# Table of Contents

# A Quiet Space

A girl walks into the library.

It is very quiet inside.

People are looking at books.

Some are working at tables

or on computers.

Watch a video here!

# A Place to Read

A library is a place to read. Many people go to the library to find a book. Reading can be for learning or for fun.

There are more than 100,000 libraries in the United States.

Learn more here!

People **check out** books
from the library. They use
their **library cards**. These
cards let them borrow from
the library.

People can take the books home. Then they bring the books back when they are done. People can also check out movies, music, and more.

# Chapter 3

# Inside a Library

Libraries have many books. The books are stored on shelves. They are organized by **genre** and **author** name.

Learn more here!

Libraries have tables where people can read or work. Many libraries have free internet that people can use. They also have computers.

People can read books on the computer. Online books are called e-books.

People can search for a book on a computer. The computer tells them where the book is located in the library. Then they can find the book on the shelves.

The Library of Congress has more than 34 million books.

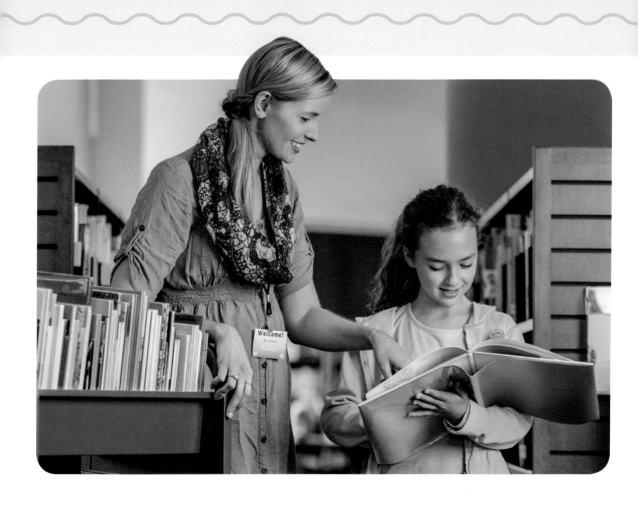

**Librarians** take care of
the books. They help people
find the right book.

People go to the librarian's
desk. They ask questions or
**check out** books.

# Chapter 4

# Sharing Information

Libraries are important

community places.

Libraries make information

available to everyone

in the community.

Complete an activity here!

Libraries are free to use. Anyone with a **library card** can **check out** books or use the library's computers.

# Making Connections

## Text-to-Self

Have you ever been to a library? What was it like? What kind of books did you see?

## Text-to-Text

Have you read other books about libraries or librarians? What did you learn?

## Text-to-World

Libraries are free to use. Why do you think that is important?

# Glossary

**author** – a person who writes books or reports.

**check out** – to borrow something from the library.

**genre** – one of several categories of books that are set apart by similar subject matter.

**librarian** – a person who organizes information and works at a library.

**library card** – a card people use to check out books or use computers at a library.

# Index

## Online Resources

# popbooksonline.com

Thanks for reading this Cody Koala book!

Scan this code* and others like it in this book, or visit the website below to make this book pop!

**popbooksonline.com/libraries**

*Scanning QR codes requires a web-enabled smart device with a QR code reader app and a camera.